Explore Rovers

Megan Harder

Lerner Publications • Minneapolis

For M.K. and A.L., with thanks

Lerner Publications Company
An imprint of Lerner Publishing Group, Inc.
241 First Avenue North
Minneapolis, MN 55401 USA

For reading levels and more information, look up this title at www.lernerbooks.com.

Main body text set in Billy Infant Regular. Typeface provided by SparkType.

Library of Congress Cataloging-in-Publication Data

Names: Harder, Megan, author.
Title: Explore rovers / Megan Harder.
Description: Minneapolis, MN: Lerner Publications Company, an imprint of Lerner Publishing Group, Inc., [2023] | Series: Lightning bolt books. Exploring space | Includes bibliographical references and index. | Audience: Ages 6-9. | Audience: Grades 2-3. | Summary: "Rovers traverse parts of space that people can't easily get to. Readers will love learning about these space machines, from their history to their current missions and where they might go in the future"—Provided by publisher.
Identifiers: LCCN 2021043252 (print) | LCCN 2021043253 (ebook) | ISBN 9781728457796 (lib. bdg.) | ISBN 9781728463469 (pbk.) | ISBN 9781728461571 (eb pdf)
Subjects: LCSH: Roving vehicles (Astronautics)—Juvenile literature. | Outer space—Exploration—Juvenile literature.
Classification: LCC TL475 .H37 2023 (print) | LCC TL475 (ebook) | DDC 629.2/95—dc23/eng/20211027

LC record available at https://lccn.loc.gov/2021043252
LC ebook record available at https://lccn.loc.gov/2021043253

Manufactured in the United States of America
1-50807-50146-11/4/2021

Table of Contents

Millions of miles from Earth,
a six-wheeled robot rolls
across Mars. It's Perseverance.
Perseverance is a rover.

Rovers are robot scientists. They explore other worlds that are hard for people to visit. Rovers can learn about the story of space, look for ancient life, and prepare us to visit other worlds.

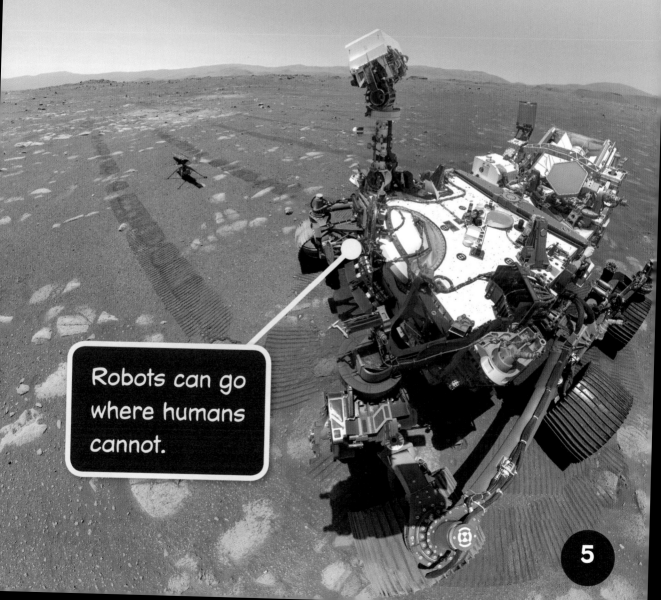

Robots can go where humans cannot.

The Story of Rovers

3 . . . 2 . . . 1 . . . *KABOOM!* The first rover ever launched did not blast off. It blew up! The rocket made to propel it into space exploded.

This rover successfully landed on the moon after the first one failed.

Scientists are always learning!

Some rovers have failed. Scientists do their best, but problems still happen. When a rover mission does not work, scientists learn from their mistakes.

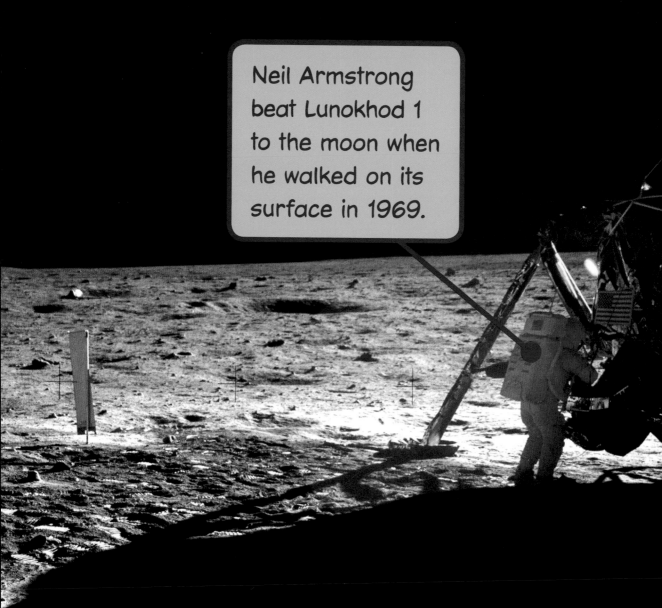

Neil Armstrong beat Lunokhod 1 to the moon when he walked on its surface in 1969.

A year after the first try, the rover Lunokhod 1 left Earth in one piece. On November 17, 1970, it landed safely on the moon.

Next, two rovers went to Mars in 1971. Both missions failed. Twenty-six years later, Sojourner became the first rover to successfully explore Mars. Between 1997 and 2021, five more rovers made it safely to Mars.

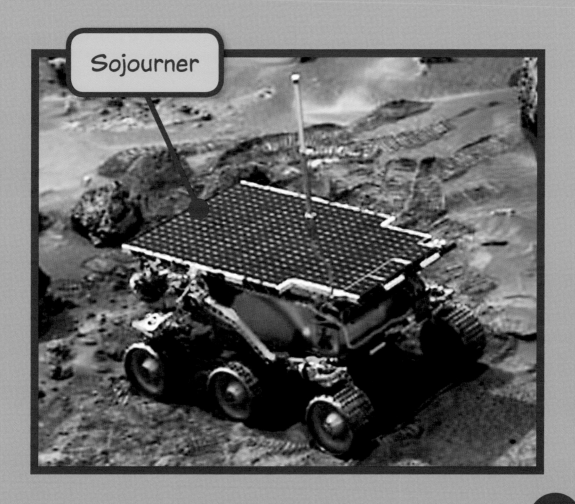

Sojourner

Rovers in Action

Rovers take pictures and videos. They collect samples. They take measurements. Rovers transmit this data to scientists on Earth.

MINERVA rovers were made to explore asteroids.

Modern rovers are still helping us learn about Mars and the moon. Rovers have even landed on an asteroid!

Perseverance arrived on Mars in 2021. It is searching for signs of past life. It will also help prepare for sending people to Mars.

Perseverance paves the way for human space explorers.

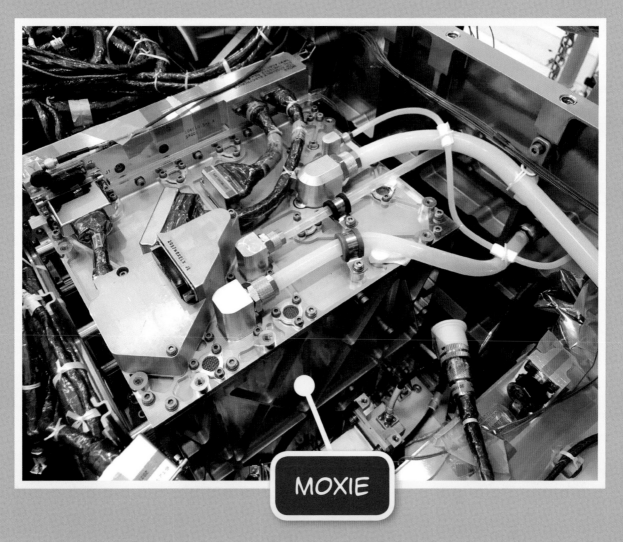

MOXIE

MOXIE is a tool on Perseverance. It can make air that people can breathe. A bigger version of MOXIE could be used to help people breathe on Mars someday.

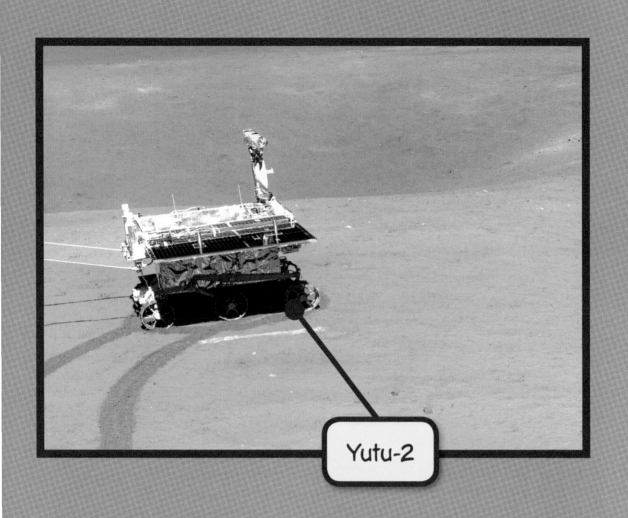

Yutu-2

Faraway planets are exciting, but our moon still has many secrets. No rover had been to the far side of the moon until Yutu-2 got there in 2019. Yutu-2 was sent to search for clues about how the moon formed.

Most rovers move by rolling on wheels. The MINERVA-II1 rovers get around by hopping! They landed on the asteroid Ryugu in 2018. The two little hoppers proved that rovers could work on an asteroid.

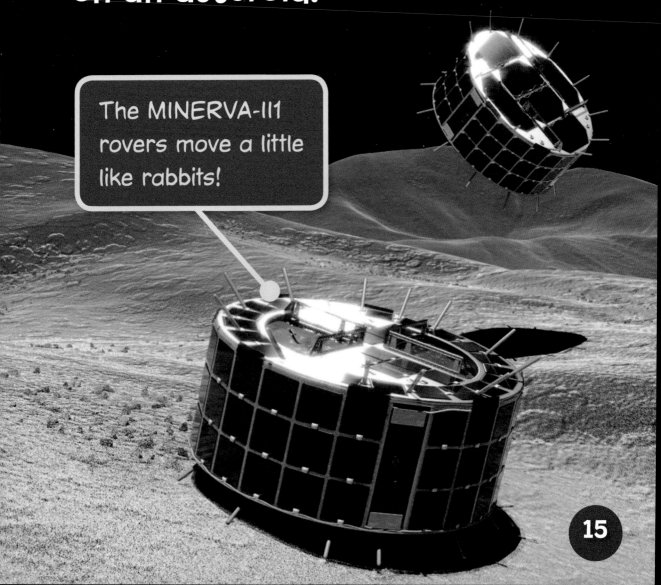

The MINERVA-II1 rovers move a little like rabbits!

Into the Unknown

Future rovers might have new tools or be built differently. They will visit new worlds and answer new questions.

A rover called Rosalind Franklin was built to take rock samples on Mars. Maybe those rocks will contain hints of past life.

One day, a rover might go to Venus. Venus is very hot. Its atmosphere is harsh. A Venus rover must be much sturdier than other kinds of rovers.

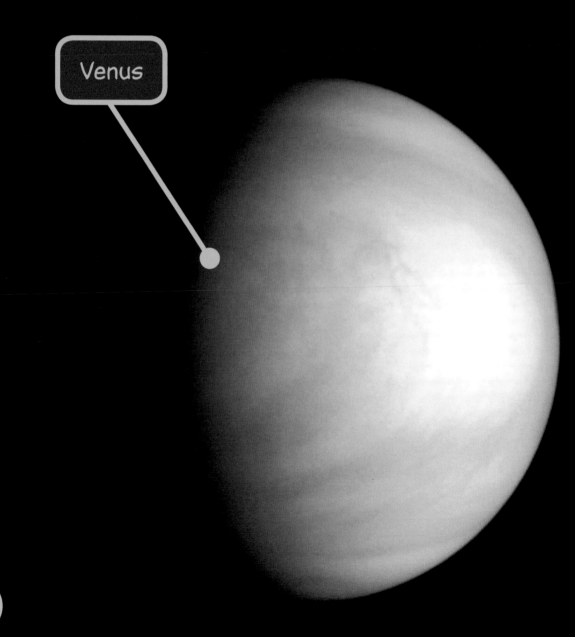

Venus

Using rovers, we can learn more than ever about space. Rovers might even help people go to Mars. Thanks to rovers, maybe you could go to Mars someday!

Rover Diagram

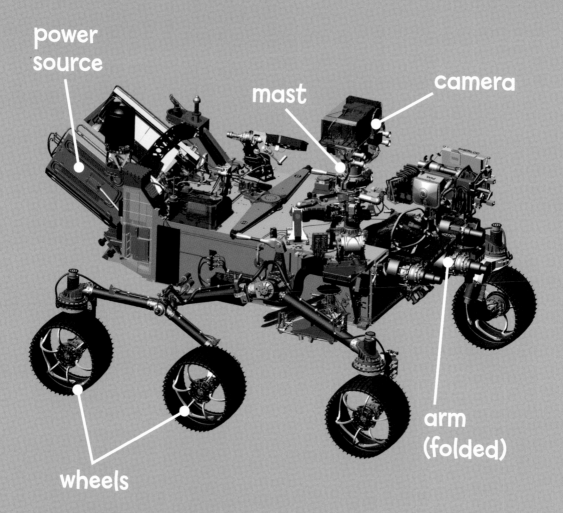

power
source

mast

camera

arm
(folded)

wheels

The Amazing Mars Helicopter

Ingenuity arrived on Mars with the Perseverance rover in February 2021. It is the first machine to make a powered and controlled flight on another planet. Ingenuity can propel itself with helicopter blades up to 15 feet (4.5 m) above the Martian ground. It can turn in midair and lower itself back down. That is not easy on a planet with a thin atmosphere! Ingenuity is a major achievement in space exploration.

Glossary

ancient: very old

asteroid: a bumpy rock in space that moves around the sun

atmosphere: the gases around a planet or a star

data: facts and information

planet: a large, round object in space that moves around a star

propel: to push or move something

transmit: to send

Learn More

Britannica Kids: Space Exploration
https://kids.britannica.com/kids/article/space
-exploration/353794

Cruddas, Sarah. *The Space Race: The Journey to the Moon and Beyond.* New York: DK, 2019.

Murray, Julie. *Rovers.* Minneapolis: Abdo Zoom, 2020.

NASA Space Place: All about the Moon
https://spaceplace.nasa.gov/all-about-the-moon
/en/

NASA Space Place: The Mars Rovers
https://spaceplace.nasa.gov/mars-rovers/en/

Schaefer, Lola. *Explore Rockets.* Minneapolis: Lerner Publications, 2023.

Index

Photo Acknowledgments

Image credits: NASA/JPL-Caltech, pp. 4, 7, 10, 12, 13, 20; NASA/JPL-Caltech/Kevin M. Gill/ flickr (CC BY 2.0), p. 5; ALEXEY RYABOV/Wikimedia Commons (CC BY-SA 4.0), p. 6; NASA, p. 8; NASA/JPL, pp. 9, 18; Norimaki/Wikimedia Commons (CC BY 3.0), p. 11; CSNA/Siyu Zhang/ Kevin M. Gill (CC BY 2.0), p. 14; JAXA via AP, p. 15; NASA/Aubrey Gemignani, p. 16; All About Space Magazine/Future/Getty Images, p. 17; NASA/GSFC/Bill Hrybyk, p. 19.

Cover: NASA/JPL-Caltech/Kevin M. Gill /flickr (CC BY 2.0).